Journey to Redemption Rock

A Story of Death, Taxes, Miracles, and Faith

Jeanette Wynecoop

Journey to Redemption Rock

by Jeanette Wynecoop

Copyright © 2025 by Jeanette Wynecoop

All rights reserved.

No part of this publication may be reproduced, distributed, or transmitted in any form or by any means, including photocopying, recording, or other electronic or mechanical methods, without the prior written permission of the author, except in the case of brief quotations embodied in critical reviews and certain other noncommercial uses permitted by copyright law.

ISBN Information

Paperback Edition ISBN: 978-1-7357503-2-3

Ebook Edition ISBN: 978-1-7357503-3-0

This book is a work of nonfiction. It reflects the author's experiences and opinions and is presented solely for informational and inspirational purposes. The information herein should not be considered legal, financial, or professional advice. Readers should seek appropriate professional guidance related to specific circumstances.

Printed in the United States of America.

First Edition: 2025

To my beloved husband, Steve, whose unwavering support and boundless love sustained me through our family's darkest hours. To our children, whose resilience and compassion served as my guiding lights. To my dear nieces and nephews, who bravely walked alongside me through heartaches and trials.

To the incredible women of my Revel Writing Group, whose encouragement kept my hope alive and my pen moving. Special gratitude to my devoted editor, whose patience and belief in this story made its telling possible.

Your collective love, strength, and understanding have been my greatest blessings.

Foreword

The line *"Is this heaven?"* from *Field of Dreams* has always resonated with me. In the film, Shoeless Joe Jackson stands on a baseball field in the middle of an Iowa cornfield, asking this profound question. The field represents beauty, peace, spirituality, and joy—so perfect it feels unreal.

I feel that same sense of wonder standing atop Redemption Rock after the three-mile hike from Redemption Rock Lodge. Here, it's impossible not to sense something greater at work, as if angels stand beside you. For me, Redemption Rock is more than a place—it's a testament to the power of dreams and the journeys they inspire.

Hiking the extra half mile to the Tower brings an overwhelming mix of peace and joy—something you want to share yet also keep sacred. The whisper from the same movie, *"If you build it, they will come,"* was an irresistible call, one that led to the creation of the lodge, the lookout tower, and ultimately, my home on our family's land in Post Falls, Idaho. This 1,100-acre mountain was almost lost to us—until my mother had a dream. That dream ignited a journey of grief, healing, and redemption.

Foreword

Standing at the summit of Redemption Rock, the vast landscape stretches before you, the air crisp with the scent of pine. Sunlight filters through the trees, casting a golden glow. It's a place where the soul feels both grounded and lifted, much like Shoeless Joe's field—offering hope and reminding us that some dreams, no matter how improbable, are worth chasing.

If this book has taught me anything, it's that dreams sustain us through life's hardships. They serve as inner compasses, guiding us toward authenticity and purpose. Letting go of them leads to a life of regret.

This story is one of perseverance, faith, and the power of dreams—both literal and figurative. For those attuned to God's calling, you will find joy in how this journey unfolds. For those seeking their own path, I hope *Journey to Redemption Rock* inspires you to pursue your dreams with courage.

Every step my mother took to save and transform this land was an act of faith. The challenges were immense, but the rewards were immeasurable. Today, the lodge offers refuge, the lookout tower stands watch, and my home symbolizes new beginnings. Redemption Rock is more than a place; it's a living testament to resilience and vision.

My mother's story is not just about saving the land; it's also about the miraculous outcome of faith and perseverance. It reminds us that every trial brings triumph, every setback paves the way for renewal, and every truth leads us closer to what is meant to be.

As you read my mother's story, I hope you find the courage to align your life with God's grace and purpose. May this book encourage you to face challenges with faith and authenticity.

Steve Wynecoop

Introduction

Ask, and it shall be given, seek and you will find, knock, and it will be opened to you.—Matthew 7:7

Many of my family and friends have asked me to write this story. Although my journey is one of sorrow and suffering that came into our lives after my sister's death, it is also a story of standing firm in faith and believing the promises of God.

There are many parties involved in this story—attorneys, the bank, the courts, and the IRS—each representing obstacles on a path toward a deeper understanding of what it means to have redeeming faith. These trials, while painful, were instrumental in revealing not just the literal meaning of redemption in our earthly world, but also the profound spiritual truth of God's redemptive power. I am excited to tell you how the Lord intervened and helped us solve the many problems we encountered in a miraculous way.

Before I share the details, I feel it is necessary for you to

Introduction

understand what I believe, to give you a better understanding of why I did the things I did in my quest for justice.

I believe the Bible is the inspired word of God. I believe Jesus Christ is the "only begotten Son of God." I believe He is our Lord and Savior, our Redeemer, and that He is alive and well and still doing His work in our world today from His heavenly kingdom. I believe He directs our path (if we ask), that He will make Himself known to all men and women (if they are truly seeking), and that we can all have this faith (if we pray and believe). "Ask and it shall be given, seek and you will find, knock and the door will be opened." (Matthew 7:7)

In many ways, as I walked through the deception for several years of my life, it felt very much like a game of football, because all the key players denied having the information that would help solve the problems of my sister's estate. I recall the first developer I contacted to try to sell the property to settle her estate's debts who said, "You are not a player in this game." Then he added, "This is not an emotional issue." *Not a player! Not emotional! Not true!* It's true I wasn't the owner of the property, but I was related to both the owners who were losing their property: one of them was my sister, who had just passed away, and the other owner was Tom, my sister's husband and my husband's cousin, who had just suffered a stroke. *How could it not be emotional?* I definitely felt like I was a "player."

The missing tax information, the legal paperwork, and the many other necessary answers that were being withheld were the football. As I approached the different parties who should have the answers, they would pass the responsibility to answer my questions—the football—to other players in the game. The key players were several attorneys, the bank, the real estate company—all who were supposed to be repre-

Introduction

senting the estate—and lastly the squatter who was trying to tie up the surveyed acreage Tom was trying to sell to pay his debts. The squatter was also trying to get a 10-acre piece by squatter's rights, by claiming adverse possession (a form of squatter's rights).

You could not see anyone in motion in this ongoing game of deception and fraud. The games of life are not always visual, but in this game—like football—fouls were made through a lot of deception. There were no referees to throw a flag. The attorneys involved were just watching it happen, as Tom was bankrupt, and some were key players in the game. The game was real but played in the shadows. The field and the intended touchdown would be getting the property for themselves.

I hope you will understand why I chose to play in this game, by investigating what was happening with the estate and the ensuing lawsuits, when I knew in my heart the cards were stacked against me, and I knew the players in this particular game of life were so much bigger than me. Again, the key players were attorneys, the bank, the IRS, and anyone who could claim to be a legitimate party in interest. I believed God was bigger than them all, and that He was leading my husband and me to help our brother-in-law, Tom.

Writing this book is my next act of devotion, ensuring that the spiritual truths and teachings of Christ that have carried me through these trials of my life might aid you in yours, and that the legal lessons I learned along the way will be of value to you. My prayer is that something within these pages will resonate with you, contribute to your spiritual growth, or at the very least help you draw parallels to the larger narrative that connects us all.

Introduction

It is with my reverence for the written word and my dedication to my faith that I offer these reflections and insights to you. My hope is that the words of this book will guide you toward the redemptive power of God's love, and that together we may continue the conversation that began with the earliest followers of Christ and continues to shape our lives today.

Chapter 1

The Phone Call We Dread

*Yea, though I walk through the valley of the shadow of death,
I will fear no evil; for You are with me ...—Psalm 23*

I reached for the phone that day with no particular thought in mind other than to stop the ringing. It was my sister, Shirley. Her usual happy voice was strangely quiet as she told me she would be coming to Redmond and asked if she could stay with us at our home. Thanksgiving was approaching, and plans for family gatherings and celebrations were in the making, but this was not why she was coming.

She had daughters in our area, but she was asking if she could come and stay with our family. This was no surprise, as we were very close. Whenever she came our way, most often she stayed with us, and whenever we went her way, we stayed with her family. I was happy to hear her voice and even happier to know she was coming.

Our families were very close, because my husband Steve was Tom's cousin, and Shirley was my sister. Both our families had lived near one another after marriage, continuing the family bond through fellowship. I also had lived with Shirley and Tom as a teenager during my sophomore and senior years of high school. So, I basically finished growing up with their kids while babysitting and taking care of them on various occasions. I became emotionally attached to them when they were babies. When they moved to Wellpinit so Tom could teach high school, I moved with them. It was natural for me to feel a sense of responsibility to try to help the kids after Shirley's death and Tom's stroke. It was also understandable that they should reach out to us for counsel in the aftermath of their parents' illness.

Our phone call took a sudden turn to horror, followed by emotional pain, when Shirley told me, "I've been diagnosed with cancer, and the doctor said I have three to five months to live." Her voice sounded strained, and I felt sure she was holding back. Dryly, she said, "I'm coming to Seattle to have exploratory surgery to see if anything can be done." She was scheduled for surgery right away. I tried to sound positive and not let her know how alarmed I was while thinking, *How are we going to face the holidays?*

A huge dark cloud of doom now hung in silence over Thanksgiving and Christmas, with all the season's good cheer and good news of God's special gift. I searched for words of comfort, but nothing came. We were both silently leaning on God as we hung up the phone. I know He must have been there because I didn't fall down. I didn't collapse in sobs as I thought about losing my big sister, my friend, and my laughter. I remember how she would always come to my house, and if I was in another room, she would call in a loud voice, "SISTER!" It was always a joy to hear her calling me. It meant we would be taking time out for laughter, taking time out to go to lunch or share the simple joys or problems of raising our children. Reminiscing on the past, I collected all the faith I could muster and began thinking positively. It wasn't over yet! There was still time; maybe God would heal her. Maybe He would do one more miracle.

How many times have we picked up the phone expecting a cheerful report or just a happy "hello," when we are suddenly and unexpectedly thrust into the middle of a family crisis? Steve's father passed away from a heart attack. Then another horrible call informed us that his brother was killed in an automobile wreck in which he was the sole occupant. Well, yes, he may have had a little too much to drink at the town festivities, and his wife had warned him not to drive. He thought he was still capable enough. But he was so young—only 34! *Why him? Why now?*

Then there was the heartbreaking call I made to my sister, Shirley. "I've lost my baby... He was stillborn! I didn't even get to hold him!" It was so sudden and so unexpected, as I wasn't full term yet, only six and a half months along. It felt like the universe had conspired to take away the thing my heart had so eagerly anticipated. It was too much! I was overwhelmed! Temporarily, I didn't feel like praying. I couldn't go to God, I reasoned, because He had the power to change things, and in this case—in *my* case—He hadn't. In the midst of my sorrow, I felt very alone and didn't really feel like God was with me.

In those dark moments, I felt very alone and abandoned; my faith was on a downhill slide, picking up speed. If only I could reach deeper into my heart like Mary and Martha, who believed their brother would be alive if Jesus had been there. They, too, faced the same moment of profound grief; their brother was Lazarus, gone before they could grasp the reality of their loss. When Jesus finally arrived, Mary and Martha said to Him, "Lord, if You had been here, my brother would not have died." (John 11:21–32). Their words mirrored my own silent lament: *if only He had intervened.*

Yet even in their grief, Mary and Martha held on to their faith. Jesus, moved by their pain and God's plan, performed a miracle by raising Lazarus from the dead. This story reminds us that even when God seems silent, He is working in ways we cannot yet see. In the end, it was the loss of our firstborn son that brought me closer to Jesus, because I realized that since our baby was in heaven, so was my heart. "For where your treasure is, there will your heart be also." (Matthew 6:21). In my sorrow, I learned that faith isn't about avoiding pain but about trusting God's love amidst it. At first, I thought I had to pray that someone would take care of our baby, as I didn't have a grasp on the greater ways of God. The Lord soon gave me the assurance in prayer that He loved him more than I, and that our baby would be well taken care of.

As I hung up the phone after Shirley's call, the flood of memories and emotions surged through me, and I began an inner dialogue of questions and answers. This is the process of faith—a wrestling match of sorts, where doubt and hope collide. It begins with the seeds of doubt. These seeds are often planted in moments of despair, moments when life tests us beyond what we think we can bear. Faith is never tested or challenged on top of the mountain, but only in the valley, at the bottom, where none of us ever want to go. There, in the valley, we have to stop and consider and evaluate what we truly believe. It is there our faith is tested and restored, or not. Thankfully, God didn't leave me there alone. It might take time, but if we hang in there and pray to God (despite our current belief that He isn't with us), He will help us. He will give us the tools to learn how to live with the cards life has dealt us. Our problems can be the exact tool

God uses. It is in these trials that we often find the deepest sense of His silent presence, whispering words of comfort and strength into our souls.

Shortly before her death, Shirley told me, "Jesus was in my room last night." I was afraid to ask, but I inquired, "What did He say?" She replied, "He was getting things ready." I'm sure He was! Didn't He say He would prepare a place for us? She didn't sound so happy, so I didn't inquire further, but I knew He hadn't healed her. *I wish now I would have asked more about it!* We didn't have the good news we wanted, and we were sad.

Shirley had a horrible time after she started chemo. Throwing up all the time, she didn't want to go anywhere or do anything. Once she asked me, "Do you think I will make it?" I skirted the answer by telling her she had to stop throwing up. *What a stupid answer!* She couldn't stop the effects the chemo was causing. Her doctor had advised us to keep a positive outlook and not talk about death. I regret that now, as I know she was somewhat afraid, but as Sisters in Christ, we could have talked about heaven and the glorious gift God has in store for us—eternal life, free from pain and suffering, and no more tears, and being together with our loved ones who had passed earlier! Yes, I'm sorry we were advised not to talk about death, for that is the doorway to eternal life and all the blessings God has promised us.

I am still sad as I remember the day I was in her room; I was lying on the floor trying to hide my tears from her. She commented that she was so miserable she couldn't even cry. I had gotten up from the floor and was sitting by her bed when she threw her arms up and shook them. At that time, she was wearing a death mask and looked so horrible that I broke into tears.

Briefly I thought that now I had an excuse for my tears, so I said, "Well, I will cry for you," and released my tears. Abruptly she said, "Well, you can stop now." I hadn't even gotten started!

Sadly, Shirley knocked on heaven's door in May of 1985, leaving a grieving family with what some would call a "probate from hell." To add to our misfortune, her husband suffered a stroke the day after her death. The executor of her will resigned shortly after she died, because he worked for the bank that was also a major creditor of Tom. To cover my sister's cancer treatments, Tom had borrowed $85,000 from that bank. The other attorney who wrote the will—a long-time associate and friend who was also named in the will as an executor—resigned from taking care of the estate for reasons I did not understand.

They said she left no will, or it was lost. They said it was an old will that had not been recorded. I know that, before her death and while she was in the hospital, Shirley made a new will, but we were told it was too soon before she died, and the will would not be valid because it was made "in anticipation of death." I never saw the new will she made in the hospital, and I never knew if this was correct legal advice. That is what Tom said his attorney told him.

Tom was in the hospital and could not attend Shirley's funeral due to his stroke. When he got out of the hospital, he went back to Spokane. He still had the blood clot in the back of his head that had caused the stroke, and Shirley's children called us many times, concerned they were going to lose their father also. We were concerned as well and contacted his attorney in Seattle to see if we could help until Tom recovered or in case of his death. So, with Tom's authorization, his attorney wrote the paperwork making me a personal representative of the estate. This gave me the authority to contact his attorneys and creditors and speak for him or ask questions. Little did we know that if Tom had died, the paperwork and authority to act for him would be voided. I also did not know the web of deception I would encounter as I talked to the attorneys involved with the estate.

I met with Tom's Spokane attorney to present him with the personal representative paperwork the Seattle attorney had created, and he told me I could not be a personal representative. He vehemently resisted the idea! But after some discussion, he agreed I could. He warned me I might get in trouble if Tom had made any mistakes. He resigned before I left his office, and I believe he knew that without an attorney to represent the estate, I would not be able to talk to the judge, as the estate was now in probate. I don't know if that's why he resigned, but it was clear he didn't want me involved. I tried several times to talk to the judge handling the case, but the judge said he couldn't discuss the case with me without an attorney.

As time went on, we became more involved in Tom's legal problems as we began assuming some of his debts. Making matters worse, we had no legal training or knowledge of what we were getting ourselves into as we paid his property taxes. The IRS had told us mortgages were first, so we allowed Tom to give us a mortgage to protect the $11,000 we had invested to redeem his land. This mortgage is what allowed us into the two lawsuits as "parties of interest," and it was the key to saving the land in not only the first lawsuit, but also the second, which was started by a timber company.

Chapter 2

A Most Incredible Dream

I am the light of the world. He who follows Me shall not walk in darkness, but have the light of life. —John 8:12

There are many ways God works with us, but I believe He sometimes works the night shift and speaks to us as we sleep by giving us a dream that is supposed to mean something or by waking us with something He wants us to remember or investigate. I had two very vivid experiences that led me to act, believing that God was the author of them.

The first experience, in April 1986, was when I had a dream about Jesus that woke me in the middle of the night, touching my soul and startling me to wakefulness. The date of the dream has special significance, because it was the beginning of the following true story and the journey into lies and deception that I would soon encounter. I would later discover that Tom's property had already been deeded to the county for back property taxes in April 1986. The property had been deeded to the county a few days before the dream.

The dream began with a night vision. It was so real that I will never forget it. I saw in the distance a great mountain. I did not know where it was or how far it was from me. There were no audible words, only a knowing that I should "follow the light." As I remember this now, it is clear that Jesus was the light I was to follow. He says, "I am the light of the world. He who follows Me shall not walk in darkness, but shall have the light of life" (John 8:12).

In the dream and my journey to the mountain, I seemed to be walking, and I had to stop several times to make sure I was "following the light." If there was light on the path ahead, I went in that direction, each time drawing nearer to the mountain and each time stopping to wonder to myself, *Where am I going? What am I doing?* Getting closer to the mountain, the climb got steeper, and I had to pull myself up with the large clumps of grass. When I had almost reached the top of the mountain, I stood at the foot of a huge cliff face that went straight up. In the dream, it got darker as I stood looking up at the climb and its steepness and wondered, *How am I going to get up there?*

Suddenly, I was surrounded by a shaft of brilliant light, and I was instantly near the top just under the edge of the rock cliff, as if I was in an elevator. Looking up, I reached for the edge of the rock to pull myself up, and suddenly above me … I saw Jesus. His jaw was clenched, and it appeared He was terribly upset. I gasped for breath, as one does when startled. My gasp was the only audible sound in the dream. *Why was He so unhappy?* I wondered silently to myself, *Why is He still suffering?* I asked myself these questions three times because I believed Him to be in Heaven with our Father God and reasoned He should be happy there.

Journey to Redemption Rock

As I stared up at Him, temporarily frozen in shock, three reasons came instantly to mind: "Still being rejected," "going their own way," and "wickedness of the world." Later I wondered, *Who, Lord? Who is rejecting You? Is it anyone in the family? Is it in the future?* I felt Jesus was communicating with me with His eyes, within my spirit. The dream abruptly ended, but the memory of it continued to haunt me. It was so real! It seemed to call for action—mine?

In the dream, I was never told if it was Tom's family, a friend, or just someone in the world who was making Jesus so unhappy. No, not in the dream or the events that followed. There were clues, but no facts! *Who was rejecting? Who was going their own way? Who was involved in the wickedness of the world?* Since I had that dream, so long ago, I have encountered many people who are rejecting Christ. I know God also knows, and whoever they are, I hope and pray they will stop going their own way and repent, because Jesus knows and cares deeply. They might even consider paying restitution if they have defrauded someone!

It saddens me to know that anyone is still rejecting Christ, with all the information we have readily available about His life, with all the prophecies that have been fulfilled with His life and death, and with all the miracles Jesus did during His life and after. Didn't He say, "You search the Scriptures, for in them you think you have eternal life; and these are they which testify of Me" (John 5:39)? You can even ask Google; even it agrees that Jesus existed, and it quotes the scriptures better than we can.

Whenever I ask my grown children a question and they don't know the answer—or they are too busy to tell me—they say, "Ask Google." So now, if I want the exact words of Christ or more information about the life of Christ and want a more immediate answer, I just ask Google. Now, when I seek answers, I ask, *What did Jesus say about this or that?* I am no longer in the dark, as Jesus continues to lead me into the light.

I cannot begin to explain the reality of this dream—how it was under my skin and in my every thought, and how it changed my heart and started me on a path I never would have wanted to take. A path whose destination I didn't know, nor when or how it would end.

The morning after the dream, I told my husband that I felt the dream had something to do with Tom Wynecoop, who lived in Spokane, 300 miles away, and I needed to go check on him. His children had been telling us they were afraid for his health, that he was bankrupt and needed money to buy medicine. My husband agreed that I should go and check. I knew Tom owned land, but I didn't know that it had unpaid property taxes or how many acres he had.

Getting to Tom's house was about a six-hour drive. I was weary but unsuspecting as I stood at the door knocking. As soon as Tom opened the door, we greeted each other, and he immediately said, "Well, I have lost the property."

"What?" "Why?" "What do you mean?" I asked.

Tom continued, "The county has deeded the property to themselves for back property taxes."

I knew Tom owned a large amount of acreage, but I didn't know at that time how many acres, or that it included a mountain with a huge rock outcropping at the top, just as I had seen in my dream. If I had seen the property in the past, I could not recall the rock at the top, for there was not a drivable road to reach it.

Journey to Redemption Rock

After going through the lawsuits and satisfying the creditors, we put in a logging road to the top and were able to finally see the mountain and the "Rock" which I had seen in my dream. The new logging road would also allow us to log some of the property to start paying off the IRS debt, which was still outstanding. The final settlement with the IRS would come years later, after they had seized the land.

Returning to the matter of paying the county back taxes: after much discussion by phone, my husband and I decided to pay the taxes owed to the county and get the land back in Tom's name. During the days that followed, I went to the county tax office, and with the help of our credit card and my husband's permission, paid the delinquent taxes due. We had to max out our credit card to around $10,000 and borrow another $1,000 from my brother Russell to bridge the gap between how much we could come up with and how much more taxes Tom owed the county for the preceding five years, 1981 through 1985.

Thinking back, it was probably crazy to max out our credit card without a financial safety net, but we truly believed the Lord was leading us, and we put our trust in Him. Tom needed our help, along with God's help, to get him out of this terrible web of debt and deception he was caught up in.

Chapter 3

Standing On Shaky Ground

Trust in the Lord with all your heart, and lean not on your own understanding. —Proverbs 3:5

As I look back now, I wonder how I had the courage to even speak to the IRS. *How did I dare to enter a lawsuit and stand before a judge having only the truth to tell, no lawyer to represent the case, and not a speck of law background?* At the root of this tax debt was a misunderstanding of the tax status of certain assets. Tom believed these assets were exempt due to his American Indian heritage. The confusion primarily centered around a mine situated on Indian land. Tom believed the income from the mine was exempt from taxation. However, this assumption was incorrect. Tom faced a substantial federal tax debt, which quickly escalated beyond his means.

The only thing I knew about taxes was that you have to pay them, and you had better do it right and on time, or there would be penalties and interest added. *If only the sage advice of Christ had been followed in this case, when He said, "Render therefore to Caesar the things that are Caesar's, and unto God the things that are God's" (Matthew 22:21).*

Tom had the understanding that when the IRS took their five-bedroom home with a view in Redmond, they would not touch his land in Idaho. My sister hoped someone in our family would buy the house, so when the IRS put it up for silent offer, we made one, which the IRS rejected. Instead, they sold it for a cash deposit of $20,000, with monthly payments, giving the buyer, an attorney we didn't know, a four-year note to pay the remaining balance. The total amount the IRS received would not count toward Tom's debt because of the four-year note. The IRS also put a lien on his land in Idaho, which was around 1,100 acres.

My goal in the beginning was to help Tom and his and Shirley's grown children. We had no idea that our family would someday become the owners of the Post Falls property, which was not only the most beautiful property but also loved by both our families and the surrounding neighbors, who wanted to keep it a secluded mountain for the neighborhood. During this awful time, I learned that when you try to rescue a drowning victim, the rescuer sometimes gets pulled under by the weight of the person drowning as they cling to them for help.

Tom's problems would soon become ours, and some of his debt would also become ours. Problems would very quickly turn to liens and lawsuits, which I felt God had warned me of in various dreams as I slept. Eventually, I would feel the similarity of my situation to that of rescuing a drowning man—someone so deeply in debt he can't be saved—as I felt myself being pulled under with Tom's debts to the county, the bank, and the IRS.

Journey to Redemption Rock

When it all began, I was happily a housewife and the mother of five children. I had had a few years of secretarial experience, but had since chosen to stay at home with our children. I loved my life as it was, and being the mother of five wonderful children was the only success I needed, with two exceptions. My husband and I had a bed and breakfast to run, and my elderly mother to take care of. So, standing up to speak before anyone, let alone a judge, was certainly not my cup of tea. Moreover, my time away from home was difficult.

Looking back on my grade school years, I remember my hands shaking whenever I had to stand up before the class and read from my own report. I never outgrew the fear of speaking before a group or a prominent person. This was especially true of a judge who had the power to make all the decisions in our favor—or not.

As I took inventory of my brother-in-law's troubles following my sister's death, and as I investigated what was going on with the estate, I could only describe it as a "probate from hell." *If I had known what I was going to encounter and the years of my life I would spend doing it, I might have prayed to God to send someone else to help my brother-in-law.* As I look back, I shake my head at myself and say there is only one reason, only one answer—and His name is God. His name is Jesus. And my dream.

In the dream I had, I saw Jesus and felt His sorrow, and I knew there was something I had to do. Before having this dream, I saw and felt my sister's pain as she spent her last days fighting cancer, hoping God would heal her. It was my love for my sister and her family and for my God that compelled me to get involved. It is my hope and prayer that my story will touch your heart, lead you to meet Christ in these pages, and inspire you to say, *I believe,* as many others have said who have encountered Him.

I am reminded of the biblical story of the Samaritan woman at the well who met Christ when she went down to draw out water for her family. First, He asked her for a drink, and she replied, "Why are you talking to me? I am a Samaritan woman, and Jews have no dealings with Samaritans." He said, "If you knew the gift of God, and who it is that asked you for a drink, you would have asked Me, and I would have given you living water" (John 4:10). She said, "You have nothing to draw with. How are you going to give me this drink?" (Sounds a bit sassy, right?) He told her He could give her living water and she would never thirst again. He then told her to go get her husband. She replied, "I do not have a husband." Christ said, "You have well said, because you have had five husbands, and the one you're living with now is not your husband." She answered, "You must be a prophet" (John 4:17).

Of course, we now know the living water He was offering was a spiritual drink for the soul. But the Samaritan woman did not recognize Him as the Messiah yet. Before she went on her way, Jesus told her He was the Messiah she had been waiting for. This was special because women did not have a voice in those days, and she was also a Samaritan—and "Jews had no dealings with Samaritans," as she noted. The great part of her story is that she did what Jesus told her to do, and when the people of the town came and talked with Him they said to her, "Now we believe, not because of what you said, but we have talked with Him ourselves." It is my hope that perhaps this story will cause you to talk to Jesus yourself—that you will believe, not because of my story or the Samaritan woman's story, but because you have talked with Him yourself, and God will give you the faith to believe. Prayer works!

Chapter 4

Redemption

Let the redeemed tell their story. —Psalm 107:2

Since this story is all about redemption, I feel the need to clarify the meaning of the word and who I think is responsible in this story. Redemption requires two distinct actions. It cannot be accomplished alone. It needs someone to do the action or for God to work through a person to do the action. In this case, I believed the Lord was working in me and through me. *Redemption is what happened.*

The first action is the process of being saved from sin, error, or evil. The second action is someone gaining or regaining possession of something in exchange for payment or the clearing of a debt. Redemption is what happened with Tom's land.

In my first visit with Tom, I discovered his debt to the county in taxes was five years past due, and the county had deeded his land to itself. At the time, I didn't know I was about to become a redeemer! It was only when I went to the tax department to find out the procedure and pay all the back taxes that I saw it on the records. It turned out that whoever paid the taxes before the land was put up for auction was called the "redeemer." This did not happen in this case, because I asked for the property to be put back in Tom's name. I wasn't trying to get his land, only trying to save it from auction. I made it clear in the ensuing lawsuits that we had paid the back taxes. After the property was redeemed, the bank started its lawsuit. I always felt in my heart Jesus was the true Redeemer and that He just used me, as my spirit was willing to be His hands and feet to do the action required for the redemption of the land, and I believed it was the right thing to do.

It was during this ordeal that I came to realize the true meaning of the words "redeemer" and "redemption." To me, this means Jesus can also redeem lost land. "For the Son of Man has come to seek and to save that which was lost" (Luke 19:10).

When Jesus walked among men, He taught that He was doing the works of His Heavenly Father and that it was His "delight" to do the will of God. He did the works of redemption, healing, and teaching on our behalf. He also did the work of redemption, whereby He purchases and ransoms us —at the price of His own life—securing our deliverance from the bondage and condemnation of sin. Paul told the Corinthians, "You are not your own, for you were bought at a price" (1 Corinthians 6:19–20).

To the Jews who believed Him and to all men (regardless of religion), Jesus said, "If you hold to my teaching, you are really my disciples. Then you will know the truth, and the truth will set you free." *Free from the bondage and lies of Satan. Free from the darkness that keeps us from seeing the truth. Free to really see our true Messiah, Jesus Christ! Free in Christ by redemption.*

Sin can bring darkness and blind us, just as the Egyptian Pharaoh was blinded to the truth until he let Moses and his people go, before he was again blinded by sin and chased after them. Sin is like an ever-increasing fog that suddenly consumes us, causing us to stumble in darkness, and we can no longer see the light or the right thing to do. Only God can open the eyes of the blind, just as Jesus opened the eyes of the blind man and blinded Paul when he was on his way to Damascus to persecute Christians. It takes the touch of God to take away or inflict blindness!

In the days of Moses, God gave His promise that He would send a Redeemer. That Redeemer was His Son Jesus Christ. Jesus said, "The Son of Man came to seek and to save the lost," and "the Son of Man came as a ransom for many." (Matthew 20:28) Jesus said, "The thief does not come except to steal, and to kill, and to destroy. I have come that they may have life, and that they may have it more abundantly." (John 10:10) His last words as He hung on the cross were, "It is finished." He "finished" the work He came here to do by dying on the cross, paying the cost of sin with His death, redeeming us back to God and saving us for eternal life. Only the perfect Lamb could be accepted for sacrifice. He was the perfect Lamb of God. I believe that's why His last words were "It is finished." It was His last work to do. The death of Christ was a ransom sacrifice and was well planned and executed by the Father, Son, and Holy Ghost. He taught His disciples this would happen and that on the third day He would rise. They didn't understand until He had risen. *Do we get it now?*

The Israelites spoke against God and Moses when they said, "Why have you brought us up out of Egypt to die in the desert? There is no bread, there is no water, and we detest this miserable food!" In response, the Lord sent venomous snakes among them, and they bit the Israelites, many of whom died. The remaining people came to Moses and said, "We sinned when we spoke against the Lord and against you. Pray the Lord will take the snakes away from us." So Moses prayed for the people. The Lord said to Moses, "Make a snake and put it up on a pole; anyone who is bitten can look at it and live." Moses did as the Lord instructed. Anyone who had been bitten by a snake and looked at the bronze snake that was lifted upon the pole lived. (Numbers 21:4–9)

Jesus also said, "As Moses lifted up the snake in the wilderness, even so must the Son of Man be lifted up, that whosoever believes in Him should not perish but have eternal life. For God so loved the world that He gave His only begotten Son, that whosoever believes in Him should not perish but have eternal life." (John 3:14–16) Jesus knew He had to suffer and die by crucifixion. He knew He must fulfill the prophecy that He would be crucified. He knew His death would pay the price of sin and be "a ransom for many." (Mark 10:45)

Christian theology refers to Jesus having the title "Redeemer." This references the salvation He accomplished by His death on the cross and is based on the metaphor of redemption, or "buying back." In the New Testament, redemption can refer both to deliverance from sin and to freedom from captivity to Satan. Jesus said, "If the Son sets you free, you will be free indeed." (John 8:36)

Chapter 5

Faith

Now may the God of hope fill you with all joy and peace
in believing, that you may abound in hope by the
power of the Holy Spirit —Romans 15:13

You must have the faith of a little child to see the Kingdom. These were the words of Christ to His listeners as they questioned Him about faith. He is suggesting how to get faith; we are to come with the attitude of children—believing, trusting, hoping with the faith of a child. After the Samaritan woman talked to Jesus, she received faith to believe and then went to get her husband. After my dream of Christ, my faith was strengthened, and I took a step of faith to follow what I saw in the dream and went to the mountain.

On another occasion, Jesus asked Peter, "Who do you say that I am?" Peter replied, "You are the Christ, the Son of the living God," to which Jesus replied, "Blessed are you, Peter, because God has revealed it to you" (Matthew 16:17). When God revealed to Peter that Jesus was the Christ, Peter was willing to follow Him, and as the scripture says, "even die for Him" (Matthew 26:35). And so it was with me; when I saw Jesus in the dream, I was ready to do anything for Him, to follow and go to the mountain or wherever He would take me. It was a dream unlike any I had ever had before or since. It was so REAL and so much like *living* it.

In the Old Testament, we read that when God called the prophets, He would sometimes ask them, "What do you see?" He had something to show them—something He wanted them to do or say. My dream also made me feel God was calling me for a purpose—a purpose which I was supposed to investigate by going to the mountain. Later, I would have many questions to ask and decisions to make based on the false information I got from the people involved with Shirley's estate. I felt I was to follow the leading of the Lord, believing (without doubting) that He was involved.

Sometimes I wish I could see things through the eyes of a child, for they definitely do not see things as we adults do. Adults take things for granted and miss the little things that children see and find exciting—perhaps because they are smaller and closer to the ground, or perhaps because adults are too preoccupied to notice. Sometimes we may overlook something very beautiful, or maybe even *someone* very sad (perhaps even a friend), because we are in such a hurry to do what we are focused on.

I remember one day walking in the garden with our granddaughter Katelyn. As we passed by the statue of the little angel sitting by the small pond, Katelyn said, "Grandma, why is that little angel sad?" Surprised by her question, I stopped to see what she saw. Here was the little angel I had purchased several years earlier and placed there by the pond, but I never saw her as sad. I saw her as thinking and praying.

I passed her many times, and I always saw her the same way. Katelyn passed her only once and saw the little angel as sad. Katelyn was sad for the angel. "Katelyn," I said, "The little angel is not sad; she is only praying."

As I contemplate this story, maybe Katelyn was right and I was wrong. Maybe, just maybe, somewhere in my garden there was actually a sad angel we couldn't see. *Was it possible Katelyn could feel the presence of the angel and her sadness?* Katelyn was about four or five at the time of our stroll in the garden, and I had been struggling with Tom's problems for many years because of the dream I had. Tom's problems were overwhelming and much too big for me. The situation was totally out of my control, and I knew only God had the power to change things. I believed in God's power, so I went forward in faith. I felt compelled to do the right thing and help the family.

What do you think? Do you think we can feel the sadness or happiness of angels? Do you think we feel God's heartbreak when we ignore His principles and go our own way? Can we grieve the heart of God when we reject His love? Can we grieve the Holy Spirit? Is Christ still suffering? My answer to all these questions is "yes," because of what I saw in my dream and because the scriptures also agree. We read that the angels rejoice over one sinner who repents. (Luke 15:10) So, if they rejoice over one sinner who repents, would they not be sad over the ones who do not?

When the scriptures say, "Grieve not the Holy Spirit" (Ephesians 4:30), and that the greatest and most unforgivable sin is to blaspheme the Holy Spirit (Matthew 12:31), it means the Holy Spirit is a living entity capable of feelings—experiencing grief, joy, anger, and sorrow. Jesus said, "God is Spirit, and those who worship Him must worship in spirit and truth" (John 4:24). God is a living spirit, capable of loving and forgiving—or not. Sometimes the sin is so great He says, "Therefore I will also deal in My fury; My eye will not spare nor will I have pity; and though they cry in My ears with a loud voice, I will not hear them" (Ezekiel 8:18). He further states, "Is it a trivial thing to the house of Judah to commit the abominations they commit here?" (Ezekiel 8:17). Yes, the Lord is angry—He is furious. Earlier, He says, "Son of man, have you seen what the elders of the house of Israel do in the dark, every man in the chambers of his imagery? For they say, 'The Lord does not see us; the Lord has forsaken the land'" (Ezekiel 8:12).

Then He said to me, "Turn again, and you will see greater abominations than these." He brought me into the inner court of the Lord's house, and behold, at the door of the temple of the Lord, between the porch and the altar, were about twenty-five men with their backs toward the temple of the Lord and their faces toward the east; and they worshipped the sun toward the east (Ezekiel 8:15–16).

Listen to the heartbreak of the Lord as He shares His feelings: "I was crushed by their adulterous heart, which has departed from Me, and by their eyes, which play the harlot after their idols" (Ezekiel 6:9). Have you ever heard the Lord say He was heartbroken? This behavior was unacceptable—to worship idols or pursue other gods!

Then He says, "They shall loathe themselves for the evils which they have committed in all their abominations" (Ezekiel 6:9). The Lord had also shown Ezekiel another room filled with all kinds of idols—"creeping things," as God called them (Ezekiel 8:10). God's first and greatest commandment was clear: "Love the Lord your God with all your heart, with all your soul, and with all your strength" (Deuteronomy 6:5). He had already warned them in the Ten Commandments,

Journey to Redemption Rock

"You shall have no other gods before Me" (Exodus 20:3). And finally, He declared, "Now the end has come upon you, and I will send My anger against you; I will judge you according to your ways and repay you for all your abominations" (Ezekiel 7:3).

Based on these scriptures, Israel had truly provoked God's anger—He had reached His limit. They had previously experienced captivity in Babylon for these same offenses. It was during this time in captivity that Ezekiel received his vision of the wheel within a wheel. He recalled, "I was among the captives by the River Chebar, the heavens were opened, and I saw visions of God... the hand of the Lord was upon me there" (Ezekiel 1:1-3). Sadly, later generations seemed to forget both their captivity and the reasons for it.

Chapter 6

Liens, Infraction, Takeover

In a dream, in a vision of the night, when deep sleep falls upon men, while slumbering on their beds, then He opens the ears of men, and seals their instruction. —Job 33:15-16

The second time I felt the Lord was trying to alert me was while I was sleeping. Something happened I had never experienced before. I had gone back home to Redmond thinking the land was now safe and would be back in Tom's name. A few nights later, these three words came to me in the middle of the night as I lay sleeping: *LIENS, INFRACTION, TAKEOVER*. At first, I didn't think it was an audible voice, because *it felt like it was in my body and not my ears*. As I think about it now, I suppose it could have been audible because I was sound asleep, but it was so loud and startled me so much that it made me jump out of bed. I stood there by our bedside, trying to make sense of what I had just heard.

None of these words were words I understood or used, except for the word *lien*. This word I knew, because when we were trying to buy a house in Redmond, the seller had put a lien on our current Bellevue house—unknown to us—even though we had paid him a deposit of $20,000 to hold the new house until we could sell ours. We sold the house right away and finished the purchase, but he did not lift the lien, and the bank would not loan us money until that lien was lifted. The seller had since moved to Yakima, so it took some doing to locate him and get him to come back and remove the lien.

So, liens I knew, but what did *infraction* and *takeover* mean, *and why was that important?* The real question was *why these words kept replaying in my mind* over the next couple of days. My husband and I decided I needed to go back to the courthouse and check the records to see if there was something important that I might have missed or needed to know. So back I went to the courthouse in Idaho, determined to uncover what God might have been warning me about.

It didn't take long before I found the answer. There were several liens against the property. One was for a small tax on timber that had been logged by a mysterious logger unknown to Tom, so he didn't know about the tax or a possible future lien. Next was an IRS tax lien of $137,000. Then there was a lien from a car dealership for a car Tom bought and paid for, but the lien had not been lifted due to the negligence of the party that had placed it or an error by the county clerk. The party who places the lien is the only one who can have it removed. There was also a fourth lien. This was from a landowner whose property was contiguous to Tom's land. He had some work done on his land and somehow encumbered Tom's land. I could never determine if this was truly an accident.

The small timber tax lien could have resulted in the county taking the whole parcel of land that was logged if the tax was not paid. However, since Tom hadn't hired the logger, he was unaware his land was logged, taxed, or subject to an additional lien. The small timber tax was about $30, which I paid on the spot. *I think the whole lien business is grossly unfair to the landowner and should be against the law if it is done secretly, without the owner's knowledge.*

This was another instance in which I began to understand that God speaks to us in ways we don't always expect. He can warn us in the quiet of the night, through dreams, through a gut feeling, or in the whispers of our own spirit. His guidance, though subtle at times, is powerful and essential if we are to stay on the path He has laid out for us. I learned that when we listen carefully, these moments of divine nudging often lead us to critical actions or decisions that will shape the course of our lives.

I never found out exactly what *infraction* referred to because I would have needed a good attorney, and I couldn't find one except my friend from high school. Months later, she earned her law degree in time to help us settle the IRS tax debt and get the squatter from one of the 10-acre surveyed lots that the bank didn't take. I believed the bank did not take those 10 acres because the squatter was on it. *I couldn't stop wondering if the bank and the squatter were working together to keep the land from selling, but I had no evidence to confirm it.* Too many suspicious events surrounded the squatter. For instance, there was the bankrupt road builder who allegedly left the road incomplete according to the squatter, and the missing boat that was supposed to be the deposit. And many unanswered questions: why did the real estate company allow the squatter to move onto the land before the earnest money agreement closed? Why did they close their office and disappear so abruptly? How did the squatter get a permit to build a pond when he wasn't the true landowner?

My friend ended her practice in Idaho and moved to another state after helping us remove the squatter from the land and settle matters with the IRS. She couldn't help us with the second lawsuit brought by the timber company 13 years later. She couldn't help us with the first lawsuit because she did not have her law degree yet. She helped us with the IRS and the squatter; for that we will be forever grateful, and we praise the Lord for her and for His help too. We also praise the Lord for the silent warning that something was wrong, that the land had been deeded to the county and was in danger of being auctioned off, and we are thankful for the nighttime alert about *LIENS, INFRACTION, TAKEOVER*.

Chapter 7

The Squatter

There they are in great fear where no fear was, for God has scattered the bones of him who encamps against you; you have put them to shame, because God has despised them. —Psalms 53:5

My attention was first drawn to the squatter by the neighbors living next to him on Tom's land in Idaho. The neighbors had purchased one of the surveyed lots Tom lost in the first lawsuit. The squatter had fraudulently begun to purchase a 10-acre surveyed lot which was also part of the 153 acres lost to the bank, but he had only signed an Earnest Money Agreement and had not completed it with a purchase and sale agreement, so it was legally tied up. His neighbors phoned me one day to tell me the squatter was polluting the creek and that they had phoned Panhandle Health and reported him. At first, I thought this might help me get him off the land, so I too called Panhandle Health, requesting them to talk to him and perhaps give him a citation for polluting the creek. *Not so lucky!* They told me, "No, if we go after anyone, it will be you.

You are the landowner, so you have to take care of it." They said it wasn't their responsibility!

So back I went another 300 miles to talk to the squatter and the real estate agent who had allowed him to move onto the land before the sale closed. The agent confirmed he had only signed an Earnest Money Agreement, but he had not followed through with the sale. The squatter said he had given the owner a $5,000 boat as a down payment, but nobody—none of the attorneys or the real estate people that drew up the contract—could tell me where the boat was. I finally found a sticky note in one of the last attorneys' files that said, *The roadbuilder got the boat*. The real estate agent told me to see Tom's Idaho attorney, who was supposed to have a copy of the Earnest Money Agreement, which I did, but the Idaho attorney denied he had a copy (more than once). I inquired again as I was leaving his office for the third time. As I stood in the doorway of his office to leave, he said, "Well I'll be darned—I guess I do have a copy," and pulled the copy off the top middle of his desk. I felt this was a deliberate show of his power over me and also his arrogance that he didn't have to help me or cooperate with me. I had shown him Tom had signed a Power of Attorney so I could help him, so he had no excuse. He was just obstinate and unfriendly from the first day I went to him seeking information about Tom.

There was another mysterious glitch in the deal. The squatter said that, according to their agreement, Tom was supposed to fix the road and hadn't done it, so he wasn't going to follow through with the purchase of the land. I had seen paperwork from the state of Idaho accepting the road as finished to their satisfaction. I did not see anything wrong with the road. It looked finished to me.

When I questioned the roadbuilder, he said he never got the boat and that he had fixed the road out of his own pocket. He said Tom now owed him for all his expenses. He said he was supposed to get one of the 10-acre surveyed lots for his work. *It seemed strange to me that a bankrupt roadbuilder would get the job of building the road.* He was very angry with me for asking to see his receipts as proof of the expenses he incurred and refused to show me any expenses. He said he wished he'd never met any Wynecoops. I never met him personally, as we had just talked by phone, and that was my last conversation with him.

The boat was never located, but I was told it was an old boat and certainly not worth the $5,000 the squatter had claimed. He said he was not going to follow through with purchasing the property, even though he had moved an old trailer onto the land. *I think he had bigger plans for the property...* because most of the neighbors said he referred to the property as *Colwell's Mountain*.

At that time, the only existing road that had access to Tom's property ran through that same 10-acre lot and had access to the rest of Tom's land, including the whole mountain. My sister, Shirley, called it *God's Mountain*, and that's what I call it too! We dedicated the land at the top surrounding the Rock to the Lord and have promised never to sell that parcel. The local people have referred to it as *The Rock*, and also *Shasta Butte*. We named it Redemption Rock after we paid all the back taxes and got it back from the county. We were the "redeemers" as far as county records were concerned, but we believed Jesus had used us to redeem it. We now have owners' rights to officially name it Redemption Rock. Thanks to Jesus, who said, "I have come to seek and to save that which was lost" (Luke 19:10).

The squatter's trailer was another problem. It was dilapidated and falling apart. The neighbors were complaining about that too, as well as the fact that he was leaving garbage and papers scattered around and was making the land an eyesore. This was the truth! We spent a lot of time cleaning up his garbage, which I felt he had left on purpose to make the land unattractive and impossible to sell. We hired my attorney friend to get him off the property and then had his trailer hauled off at our own expense to the tune of $4,000 plus attorney fees. It had to be hauled off in pieces because it was so old and falling apart.

At the time of the lawsuit, the squatter was in jail for a different offense, so we had to sue him while he was in prison. He had one of his buddies continue to squat for him in his trailer, to keep his squatter's rights going. *How his friend could stand to live there in that trailer, I could not understand.* Part of the ceiling was falling, it was moldy, and it had so many other problems I can't begin to describe. The trailer was old and ugly and needed to be gone to get the land ready for an honest buyer. I suspected the squatter's friend only pretended to live there to keep squatter's rights going. *I'll never know!* I never met or saw him in person either, but it seems to me squatter's rights benefit criminals and not the landowners who are paying the taxes.

I think our government should abolish squatter's rights and make squatting on someone else's property a prosecuting offense, with help for the landowner from the local authorities. In other states, squatter's rights are even worse for the landowner. I recently saw on TV that in Oregon, if you have a house vacant or up for rent, a squatter can move in and have electricity hooked up in his name, and the police won't be able to tell if it's legitimate to make him leave, so he can continue to squat, forcing you to sue him to get him out of your house. It is called a civil matter. It should be called a criminal action, and our legislators should change the laws to help the landowners instead of squatters stealing land.

The squatter was a great security risk, and I was a bit afraid of him. My nephews, Tom and Todd, told me he once had threatened them with a gun and told them to get off his property. The nephews were not on the 10-acre piece he was squatting on. They were on the road running through his and other surveyed lots, which was their father's land. Concerned, I reached out to a judge whom I thought was a family friend and was also handling Tom's probate case in Washington, but he told me he shouldn't even be talking to me and that he could not help me. He did refer me to another attorney whom I will nickname Mr. Shotgun because he blew me away with his attitude and declined to help me talk to a judge.

Chapter 8

Lies, Obstacles, And Decisions

Woe to you also, lawyers! For you load men with burdens hard to bear, and you yourselves do not touch the burdens with one of your fingers.
—Luke 11:46

In the process of following the judge's advice to get another attorney to present the case to the presiding judge, things took another downward turn. I was sitting in the office of Mr. Shotgun, whom the judge had recommended, and was trying to hire him to take Tom's case, but he became very unfriendly for no apparent reason.

As I gave him the facts of the case, he kept leaning across his desk toward me, in a demanding way, as he raised his voice and charged, *Who's Tom Wynecoop? I'd like to meet Tom Wynecoop. Why are you here? What do you hope to get out of this?*

I continued trying to explain who I was and why I was there. "This is my sister and her husband's case, and I am trying to help them because Tom had a stroke and my sister is dead. There are no attorneys to talk to the probate judge, and all the previous attorneys have resigned, so we can't talk to the probate judge." All the while, he kept leaning toward me and loudly demanding again, *"Who is Tom Wynecoop? I'd like to meet Tom Wynecoop."*

By then, I had a few tears flowing, so he softened his voice. I can't remember how long he continued his unfriendly manner, but it was something I didn't expect, and it seemed to go on for far too long. He finally calmed down and agreed to take the case, and began to type a document. I assumed it was something he was going to present to the probate judge.

At that point, he told me I would have to promise that none of Tom and Shirley's children would attend the hearings. I had been trying to make sure the court knew they existed and saw them as possible heirs, so I did not think that was right, and I told him I couldn't agree to that. He tried to convince me otherwise, and I said, NO; I could not agree to that.

He then jerked the paper he'd been typing on out of his typewriter and told me he would not represent the case. He angrily tore the paper up in front of me. After he tore up the document, I left his office in tears and silently wept most of the drive back to Redmond, as I remembered his actions and his mean demeanor. I was shocked and overwhelmed by his behavior. *Now I know why some attorneys give others a bad name,* and why some are referred to as sharks.

Obstacles and decisions that were painstakingly made in the past continued to lead me further into the courts of law. Honestly, none of us really know where the paths of our lives will take us. That is why it is so important to choose carefully. Sometimes even the little decisions end up being life-changing ones. Following my dream was definitely a life-changing decision for me that will continue to affect both our families forever.

Journey to Redemption Rock

Speaking of little life-changing decisions, I remember a time when I asked my daughter to go with me to a wedding to serve a church friend's wedding cake. She didn't really want to go because she was suffering a broken heart at the time. Thankfully, she changed her mind, and while serving the wedding cake, she met her future husband. He was one of the wedding guests and a friend of the bride. He asked my daughter to attend the private party after the reception, and love was in the air. They were married sometime later.

Wherever this path leads, I am confident that everything will be okay because I believe in God. I believe that Jesus Christ is the Son of God and the Redeemer of the World, and I believe the dream was His way of calling me to help Tom and also to show me His heart of suffering, just as He showed Ezekiel His broken heart about the Israelites worshiping idols and the sun. I believe the scriptures teach us that angels are His messengers, whether we see them or not. I believe He leads us when we ask for His help. That He is in control, and that there is a bigger picture which we cannot now see. "He is the author and finisher of our faith," (Hebrews 12:2) and "He will keep that which we have committed until that great day." (2 Timothy 1:12) I believe God will keep giving us, and you, the seeds of faith to share with others when our storehouse seems empty.

Chapter 9

First Lawsuit With The Bank

And if children, then heirs—heirs of God and joint heirs with Christ, if indeed we suffer with Him, that we may also be glorified together. —Romans 8:17

Sitting in the court with my two nieces was a very scary moment. I had encouraged them to make an appearance, because I wanted the court to recognize them as the heirs to my sister's estate. I had read in the paperwork filed by Tom's attorneys that there were no heirs —probably because she left everything to Tom, to our knowledge. *I could not understand why his attorneys were doing this,* as the estate was about to be lost, and I wanted the court to know Tom and Shirley's children existed, in case it meant anything. We knew nothing about what to expect as we sat in our chairs waiting for the judge. Suddenly, he was there, and we knew by watching the attorneys we were supposed to honor him by standing, which we did.

He looked very imposing and full of authority in his black robe as he first addressed Annette, *Who are you and why are you here?* he demanded. Annette stated her name and that she was Tom Wynecoop's daughter. The judge quickly replied, *Well, you cannot speak for your father.* And then he turned to Denise and asked, with the same stern voice, *Who are you and why are you here?* Bless her heart, Denise could only repeat to him the very words Annette had just said. She spoke her name and said, "I am Tom Wynecoop's daughter." To which he again replied, *Well, you cannot speak for your father.* And then it was my turn!

Who are you and why are you here? I was extremely nervous, and I was glad I was sitting down as I stated my name. Trembling, I replied, "Your Honor, I have a mortgage on the property." He then held up a file folder containing some information I had written to the court. As he waved it above him, I felt he was scolding me for my writings and my presence. *Due to my fear of the proceedings and what I was supposed to say, I couldn't be sure what his intent was, but I knew he was making me very uncomfortable!* Everything was going so fast, and I had to speak up! My voice shook as I repeated, "I have a mortgage on this property." To my relief, he said, "Well, if you have a recorded mortgage, you are a party to this case, and the bank will have to file an amendment, naming you as a party, but at this hearing you cannot speak. You can speak at the next hearing."

This was good and bad news at the same time, because I had driven 300 miles to be there and would drive the same 300 miles to return home. I thought to myself, *When will the next hearing be held, and will I be notified? Will the bank's attorney once again intentionally not send me a notice?* Plus, *it would be a total of another 600 miles to drive, and what would the weather be like?* Would there be snow on Snoqualmie Pass—winter was approaching.

I had learned of this hearing through Tom's son, who had read his father's notice of hearing and decided we needed to know about it. I am grateful he did, because in doing so, he helped us save the land—at least for a time.

The bank's attorney admitted that I did have a recorded mortgage. By that admission, it was clear he knew that was the case and had given me no notice of the hearing, even though I was a "party of interest" to this lawsuit. The judge continued to reprimand him somewhat, and I think he told the judge he was sorry. *I can't be sure because I was so nervous at the time.* Their words were not making sense and were all too legal! Abruptly, the hearing was over!

The blessing and good news of that hearing was that I was there; I had a mortgage, and because of it, I was able to temporarily stop the foreclosure in process, but not at the hearings that were yet to be held. I learned the hard way that if you are called to a hearing and do not attend or send someone other than an attorney to represent you, you automatically lose. Tom's two daughters were there, but Tom wasn't, and although his daughters were present, the judge denied them the right to speak because, "They couldn't speak for their father."

I had been able to tell the judge Tom's attorneys were also representing the same bank that was foreclosing in this lawsuit. In the law, this is known as a "Conflict of Interest," but it was not a good enough argument, or *I didn't know how to follow through with it.* Another attorney had advised me of this and quoted the appropriate case law, but said he couldn't represent this case.

Without an attorney to represent him, Tom lost the first lawsuit and also 153 prime acres that he had surveyed and divided into 12 ten-acre lots. Because I was there with a recorded mortgage, the judge granted a partial summary judgment, but he only allowed the bank to foreclose on the 153 acres and not the total of 1,100 acres.

Tom had a law background but did not graduate from law school. Tom did not attend these hearings to try to help himself, because he believed that "only a fool would represent himself." When I attended the first hearing, it was because it was our only chance. *I would be that fool!* It became one small victory for "the fool," as I was able to save most of Tom's land, temporarily.

We had tried to hire attorneys, but they wouldn't represent us or Tom because he owned the land and was bankrupt. Shirley had passed away in 1985, and I believe Tom no longer cared what happened to either himself or his land. He had given up!

At this hearing, I was able to present that we had a "recorded" mortgage on the land and had redeemed the land from the county. There were still about 950 acres left after that lawsuit. We praised the Lord for His guidance and support through this awful lawsuit and were thankful for the land that was saved, and grateful only 153 acres were lost.

Later, at the foreclosure auction on the steps of the courthouse, the bank's first bid bought the property for $80,000, leaving me with tears of disappointment. Their purchase gave them the right to put all the surveyed lots up for sale. I attended the auction but was not able to bid against the bank, so they won hands down.

Previously, there had been another auction on the courthouse steps (which I attended), but somehow it was called off or postponed. *I knew I hadn't made a mistake of the date, because another couple was also there to bid.* It always puzzled me why the auction was cancelled. I know the bank wasn't there to bid at that auction, because I was there along with the other couple. *I am still suspicious of why the auction was called off.*

My mom was about 88 years old at this time and was living with my husband and me, and I had her with my sister so I could attend the auction. In the middle of the night after I returned home, sadly she fell down the steps from her bedroom on the second floor. She was disoriented because my sister had a house with one level, and we had a three-story house. Her bathroom was to the left of the bedroom in my sister's house, and in our house it was on the right. We heard the horrible loud thud as she fell from the top to the bottom of the stairs, hitting her head and breaking her cheekbone in the process, and immediately called 911. I think she also damaged her back in the fall, because she always walked a bit crooked after that. Fortunately, she lived. Unfortunately, she had to be hospitalized and was never quite the same again.

Chapter 10

Second Lawsuit By Timber Company

My brethren, count it all joy when you fall into various trials, knowing that the testing of your faith produces patience.
—James 1:2-3

In the second lawsuit, we thought we had a fighting chance because we still had the mortgage Tom had given us on the 1,100 acres. It was on record that we had redeemed part of the property from the county for back taxes, and Tom had deeded the property over to us for the $11,000 we paid, instead of letting it be lost in the first lawsuit initiated by the bank to cover his debt to them. He was tired of the IRS harassing him, and just tired of all the problems with lawsuits. He still didn't want to go to the hearings. With the IRS hot on his tail, the bank *stipulated* the IRS into the first lawsuit (whatever that meant, because I never found out). The IRS never filed anything in the court filings. Perhaps they contacted the bank directly, but they never made an "appearance" in court, so I assumed their interests would be resolved alongside with the bank's in the first lawsuit.

After losing the 153 acres to the bank, we believed Tom's debt to the bank was paid, and we no longer had to worry about losing the land again. The county was satisfied that the back taxes were paid, and the bank was satisfied with the judgment against Tom. *We couldn't have been more wrong!* We didn't know the bank had sold their mortgage, which included all the rest of the land, to a large timber company. *This is why we had to go through the second lawsuit 13 years later.* We didn't know the IRS had not released their interest in the land either, even though they were "stipulated" into the first lawsuit by the bank.

As I mentioned earlier, *we thought we had a chance in this second lawsuit because we were now the owners of the land and could hire an attorney.* We hired an attorney my friend (the one who had become an attorney and represented us in the lawsuits with the squatter and the IRS) recommended, and he assured us that Idaho's six-year statute of limitations meant we had a good case. However, I did not feel that attorney effectively argued on our behalf in the hearings that followed. He was there in body, but did not indicate to me he was trying to win our case. When I asked him to mention some of the facts of the first case that might have helped us, his reply was that *"it would only make the judge mad."* It was now 13 years later, and a different judge. I didn't know if the new judge knew any of the facts of the first lawsuit. To my knowledge, my attorney did not mention our mortgage and how we had redeemed the land from the county for back taxes. He did not mention the 13 years of interest this lawsuit was asking us to pay for Tom's debt. Even though Idaho had a six-year statute of limitations, which should have helped win this lawsuit, the court allowed California law to apply. *I don't even know if my attorney mentioned the 153 acres the bank foreclosed on earlier to pay their debt!*

Instead of the original $85,000 loan that Tom owed, which had been satisfied when the bank took 153 acres, the timber company now demanded $300,000. This amount included 13 years' interest on the mortgage they had acquired from the bank against the remaining land. I couldn't believe the extent of the injustice that seemed to unfold before my eyes. It wasn't just that we were in legal trouble—it felt like we were fighting against forces intent on burying us deeper into debt. Despite our efforts and our trust in the legal process, we lost the second lawsuit.

Losing was a crushing blow. I had believed in our case and that the truth would prevail. *I thought if the court knew the full story, it wouldn't allow foreclosure.* But even though the truth was on our side, we didn't have the kind of money required to fight back or satisfy the lawsuit. *I never thought we would lose because of what I believed were shady or possibly criminal actions.* I thought if the court knew the truth, they would not allow this foreclosure.

Since we did not have the necessary funds available, we modified and increased our loan on our bed and breakfast with a different bank. Our daughter and her husband agreed to lend us $100,000 to help satisfy the lawsuit. To stop the foreclosure by the timber company, we paid them off and were now $300,000 in debt with an updated and increased mortgage. It was after this that the IRS seized the land.

I am comforted by the words of our Heavenly Father, who tells us, "Consider it pure joy, my brothers and sisters, whenever you face trials of many kinds, because you know that the testing of your faith produces perseverance." (James 1:2–3)

Chapter 11

The Offer In Compromise

For all the promises of God in Him are Yes, and in Him Amen, to the glory of God through us. —2 Corinthians 1:20

After the second lawsuit was settled, Tom was still in debt to the IRS for a federal tax debt of $1.2 million, which had increased from the original federal tax debt due to a later audit. In my previous discussions with the IRS, they had informed me that Tom must submit an Offer in Compromise. This was the only way they would or could consider the matter. This meant I would have to hire an attorney to submit the "offer," and after receiving it, they would decide whether to accept or reject it. *No promises were given, but it was a chance.* When I contacted another attorney to submit the Offer in Compromise for Tom, I still had high hopes that his IRS debt could be reduced or resolved.

I had contacted the IRS before, when the property was still in Tom's name, without success. I asked if we could sell some of the timber, or deed property to them to satisfy Tom's debt.

Their answer was always, *"No, we have an interest in all of the property,"* and *"It would not be in the best interest of the government."* Now, the IRS was asking for an "Offer in Compromise," leading me to believe they would be willing to take less than the $1.2 million they were now saying Tom owed them. Later, it would be clear to me this was false hope and a way of dragging the situation on.

Doing as the IRS asked, I decided to contact a friend's son who was an attorney. He was a Christian, and I thought, since he was my friend's son, he would be fair and understanding and able to get Tom a reduced amount. Since Tom was bankrupt, we had to give the attorney some money up front, out of our own bank account, with a promise to pay him an additional amount for his time. That seemed fair, and we complied. It was also necessary for Tom to give him a Power of Attorney to speak to the IRS for him, which he did.

I showed the attorney what paperwork I had and explained what I believed to be true: Tom did not defraud the government. He hadn't purposely avoided paying taxes, because the income derived was from Midnight Mines on the Indian reservation. As a member of the tribe, Tom believed he did not have to pay taxes on money he received from the mine on the reservation. The tax debt Tom had was all due to what he received from the mine, and not tax avoidance. *His claim was legitimate; it was legal.* The attorney agreed to accept the case and said he would file the Offer in Compromise, and we waited several months for the wheels of justice to work and to get the hoped-for decision from the IRS.

We finally got their decision, but not before hearing rumors that they intended to reject the offer. *I dismissed the rumors as having no merit,* believing no one could know what the intentions of the IRS were because we had heard nothing. I do not

Journey to Redemption Rock

know for sure who these rumors came from, but I was contacted by an attorney I did not know who said he had someone who wanted to buy the land and would give me $200,000. We said "No," because we knew the land was more valuable than that, and that would not be enough to settle the IRS situation. We were in the middle of the Offer in Compromise and *wanted to wait for an answer from the IRS*. Plus, the land was now in our name, which meant we would be responsible for new taxes of an undetermined amount. In response, the attorney tried to make me feel guilty by saying *I 'wasn't a very good Christian'* for refusing to sell to his buyer.

He said a lot of other stuff trying to force his will on me that *didn't make sense, and I resisted*, believing I was doing the right thing by waiting for the *Offer in Compromise* to go through. The IRS said Tom needed to do that, and I was following their direction. I suspect that the attorney representing the buyer was the same one who had claimed the IRS would reject the offer. *I wondered how he also knew that I was a Christian, how he knew so much about this case, and who the mysterious interested buyer was.*

When the final decision came through, to my dismay, it was exactly what I had been warned to expect. The IRS decision was, "No." *I thought their reason was very odd!* They said our attorney had submitted the offer on the wrong form, and he would have to submit it again on the correct form. I had a hard time believing he could have done that, a hard time accepting their decision, and a hard time understanding why Tom would then cancel the Power of Attorney for the attorney we had hired to resolve his taxes.

We had hired him for Tom's sake, but Tom had to give him the authority. Now, the attorney we hired to submit the Offer in Compromise informed us that he could no longer represent Tom because Tom had canceled his Power of Attorney. Without this authorization, the attorney had no legal ability to discuss Tom's tax debt with the IRS. We were now indebted to this attorney for $3,800, and Tom canceled his Power of Attorney without informing us. I could only guess what Tom's motives were for doing this. *I think he was tired of waiting for the compromise to go through, and secondly, he was mad their decision was "No" and that the attorney had filed with the wrong form and it would have to be done again.*

Communications with Tom were difficult because we were 300 miles apart, and he didn't like talking on the phone—especially to me, because I was a woman. He didn't have a high regard for women, and since I was a woman with no legal authority or knowledge, he didn't believe I could help him.

Whatever his reasons were, I was now angry with the attorney for using the wrong form (if he really did), for the other attorney's interference, for the IRS's unwillingness to accept the compromise, and for the $3,800 we now owed this attorney. *I decided I was done trying to help Tom,* as now I was also disappointed, angry, and frustrated with him and deeper in debt. I felt Tom could have at least told me he intended to cancel the attorney's Power of Attorney.

For several months, I gave up and decided I had to stop trying to help Tom. We were another $3,800 deeper in debt, I was emotionally exhausted, and *I did not know what to do next.* I had to stop trying to get help from anyone. I was going under emotionally and financially, so I just quit trying to talk to anyone.

Chapter 12

Tax Amnesty

*Render to Caesar the things that are Caesar's, and
unto God the things that are God's. —Mark 12:17*

As soon as all the lawsuits were over and the Offer in Compromise had been denied, the IRS seized the property. *I felt sure it was an illegal seizure* and tried to decide who I could turn to. In my search for an attorney to talk to the IRS regarding the seizure, I heard about Daniel Pilla, a tax litigation consultant, who might be able to help. So I gathered what courage I could muster and, with high hopes, I made the phone call to him. To my regret, he said he couldn't represent me in court, but he recommended I buy his book, *How to Get Tax Amnesty*. I quickly followed his advice and bought the book, and after reading it, felt it would greatly benefit us in dealing with the IRS.

Experience had taught me it would do no good to contact the IRS directly. I knew I would need to hire another attorney. I reflected on all the attorneys I had contacted and decided I couldn't trust any of them except my good friend Paula, who had recently earned her law degree. I contacted her and told her about Daniel Pilla and his book on tax amnesty and asked her if she would read it. I had already confided in her about the tax problems and seizure. She agreed to look at the book, so I didn't waste time mailing the book to her.

After reading it, she agreed to contact the IRS. At that time, the case had moved up the ladder to the U.S. Attorney General and, between the two of them, a meeting was scheduled for us to meet with another IRS agent to arrange a settlement. The Attorney General wanted this case settled immediately and said it was "one of the oldest cases on the books (not settled), and it would be an act of God if it was ever settled." *I thought her comment was comical,* as my heart was telling me God had intervened and this was truly "An Act of God."

Of course, we were nervous and apprehensive as we waited. We hadn't been too successful in the past, and the IRS had never been friendly or eager to help us with any of our previous conversations about Tom's problems. We knew they had all the power on their side. They held all the right cards and could refuse to negotiate. But since we now had an attorney I trusted, we were a bit more confident.

The day finally came, and to my surprise, the IRS agent's attitude was different; he was more willing to listen and was not so cocky. He didn't act like he didn't have to talk to us. He agreed the IRS had seized the property after the 10-year statute had expired, but said that since they (the IRS) had spent a lot of money on the case "they wanted something." He warned us they could tie this case up in federal court for a couple more years, so my husband conceded and offered $25,000 to settle it, which we would pay by logging some of the trees. The agent accepted what we offered. Needless to say, we were greatly relieved, but not happy!

We had spent a lot of time and incurred substantial expenses in attending all the hearings, from court costs to travel expenses, not to mention the years of paying property taxes and the $11,000 in unpaid back property taxes we paid in the first place. We had already redeemed the land from the county years earlier in 1986.

I honestly felt we were defrauded by the IRS, the bank, and the timber company, but because we redeemed the land, it was still available for all of them to foreclose on it later. *I did not feel like we should have to offer anything. I felt cheated!* They were the ones that failed to collect in the time the law allowed. They were the ones who refused to negotiate with me earlier—years earlier—and now we were the ones being forced to pay (or risk having it tied up for more years in federal court). *It didn't make sense to me! It didn't seem fair!* But then, as I reasoned, life is sometimes not fair!

Who am I to complain about taxes, expenses, or what this has cost me? Jesus gave everything He had for you and for me. Yes, these lessons I learned were costly and not fun, but what I ultimately learned was the cost of Redemption—what it cost me, what it cost Jesus! I will be eternally grateful, because I hope to be one of the ones "redeemed" because I believed and not because I earned or deserved it!

I recall when Peter was imprisoned for preaching the gospel of Christ. There was an earthquake that miraculously freed him, and the astonished jailer asked Peter, "What must I do to be saved?" Peter replied, "Believe on the Lord Jesus Christ, and you will be saved, you and your household." (Acts 16:31) Also, "That if you confess with your mouth the Lord Jesus and believe in your heart that God has raised Him from the dead, you will be saved." (Romans 10:9)

Chapter 13

My Wilderness Experience

Who is this coming up from the wilderness, leaning
upon her beloved? —Song of Solomon 8:5

Have you ever gone through a time in your life that could be described as a "wilderness experience," when things around you seem to be falling apart and you feel lost and do not know what to do? My life during these years felt like a wilderness experience, as I leaned on God for help and direction—just as I did again when we sold our bed and breakfast in Redmond. But before I tell you how we sold it, let me share how we found it!

Our house was very special to me, as I believed God made it possible for us to buy it in a miraculous way. When I found it, we were thinking of building an English Tudor house, as existing homes were too expensive. *I felt the Lord nudge me* to inquire with a man who lived on the creek on Avondale Road in Redmond if he knew of anyone selling creekside property nearby. He said, "No, but there is an English Tudor for sale just up the road."

I immediately drove to the place he recommended, which was three houses away. It had a long driveway, about 700 feet, with a bridge across the creek. As I approached, I saw that it was indeed a beautiful English Tudor, and I was immediately in love with it, and my heart was saying, *This is it!*

As I approached the creek in front of the house and drove across the bridge, my heart fell, as I knew this house was way over our budget. To my disappointment, the owners were not at home, so I could only imagine how beautiful it was inside. *Wondering how I was going to talk my husband into coming to see it, I peeked through the side door windows.* It was everything I could wish for and way more.

Disappointed that the owners were not there to show me the inside, I returned to my car and put the key into the ignition to start it. *To my surprise, the motor would not turn over. Nothing! Not even a click!* I thought it was completely dead! Since I couldn't start the car, Steve had to come and get me. He saw that the house was the English Tudor of our dreams—the house that we were thinking of building—and it even had the creek running through it that we were hoping to find. My second surprise happened when Steve got in the car and it started right up! *Was this somehow my mistake, or was it God's plan to have Steve see the house?*

After seeing the house, my husband was interested but not convinced we could afford it. We made an appointment to see the house a few days later. However, as I had guessed, it was not within our price range, and we told the owners we loved it but would have to think about it. A few weeks went by, and my husband called me from work and told me to call the owners and tell them our answer was "NO." There was another couple looking at it, and he didn't want to keep the owners waiting. I was heartbroken as I made the call and told the owners we loved the house but *couldn't afford it.*

As I hung up the phone, *I prayed, "Lord, if the house was intended for us, You would have to talk to my husband through another man."* I knew my two cents were not going to matter anymore. Steve came home for lunch that same day and told me, "I've changed my mind. We are going to buy the Tudor." Perplexed, I asked, "What changed your mind?" He said he was talking to a guy at work who was very successful in investing, and "he told me it was a good investment." *God had heard my silent prayer as I hung up the phone.* I hadn't seen an "investment." I'd seen a future "home!"

The man especially liked the fact that the property was a Tudor with creekside property. We had recently received an unexpected dividend of $10,000 from our stock, which we could use as a down payment, and we made our offer ahead of the other couple, who were waiting for their house to sell. Our son Steve teases me, saying that this house was a miracle, and getting the land in Idaho was a second miracle. He thinks I should only expect two miracles. *I'm not so sure, for the Lord has saved my husband's life more than once.*

After 43 happy years in our dream home, we decided we needed to downsize. We discussed the pros and cons of selling the house with our nephew, Nick, who was a real estate agent, and eventually hired him to work with us. He listed our beautiful bed and breakfast for sale in September of 2020. I wasn't really prepared to sell yet, but we were getting older, and the work of cleaning, cooking, gardening, and management were becoming less manageable—*and we were in our 70's.* We still enjoyed meeting and visiting with the guests, so it made the thought of selling harder.

I didn't feel ready to retire yet, but my nephew Nick and our family convinced me the time was right. Real estate prices were up, and since our house was a unique English Tudor on 3½ acres with a creek running through it, and the grounds were very beautiful, Nick felt it would be easy to sell.

Behind the bed and breakfast, we had created a pond with a lovely white gazebo beside it. We also created a nature trail with a pergola sitting area at the end of the trail, surrounded by several blue hydrangeas. It was our own piece of heaven on earth, and we had lived there 43 wonderful years. *My heart had taken root with all the plants and dream projects we made through those years, so you can imagine how tied I was to the house and grounds.* Being a woman, I might have become more attached than Steve, so I shall not speak for him.

However, Nick convinced us the market was right, the property was still very beautiful, and it should be easy to sell. Within three days, Nick had three buyers interested, and it became a bidding war. We were thrilled when the highest bid was $100,000 more than the listing price.

The bad news was Covid-19 had just recently started, so the estate sale we were hoping to have was nixed, because people wouldn't want to enter the house. We had a lot of really nice furniture we couldn't sell and had to leave behind, including a beautiful 100-year-old antique piano that was still in immaculate shape. My heart was broken, especially for the antique piano which had belonged to my sister Shirley.

Tom and Shirley had sent it to a piano shop, as it had a problem staying in tune. There it stayed for a couple of years, as they moved to Post Falls and couldn't afford to fix it. Tom gave it to me after Shirley passed away, thinking he would lose it to the piano shop for storage fees. While it was there, we had it re-strung so it would sound as beautiful as it looked. It had beautiful carvings on the body and legs; it was truly beautiful! We couldn't take it with us when we sold, because we were downsizing into a small two-bedroom apartment. Our grown children and Shirley and Tom's family did not have a place big enough for it or could not afford the moving fees.

After the house was sold, we had nowhere to go because of Covid. The retirement community where we planned to move had closed its doors to new residents. Since we were now out of house and home, we decided to visit our daughter Missy and Dave, her husband, in Stanley, Idaho.

We were only there a few days when I had my first stroke in October of 2020. While visiting them, I was able to write part of this story, and *I am so glad, because my second stroke followed one month later, in November of 2020.* This stroke was a little stronger and affected my legs badly—for a few days I couldn't lift my legs off the floor. It also affected my speech, as well as typing and writing. Both strokes have compromised my short-term memory, but did not affect my long-term memory, for which I am very thankful to God. I am still able to recall most of the events to write this book, even if doing so is a very slow and difficult process.

Since my memory of the events is not quite as vivid, I will just say it was a terrible time in my life, and once again *I needed to lean on the Lord for direction and help* with getting this book finished, edited, and hopefully published.

As mentioned earlier, the troubles began with the death of my older sister 37 years ago in 1985. Wow! That's a long time to try to write this story. The battle to save the property took many years and two lawsuits. Going through the lawsuits caused a lot of stress, as did selling our bed and breakfast, so I can't help believing the stress of it all may have contributed to my strokes. I'm grateful to God that He helped me get through it all. Although it was not fun at the time and very difficult, it was all worth it. Perhaps surviving my strokes was also a miracle; only God knows! I will tell you more about building "Redemption Rock Lodge" on the property we saved in a later chapter.

Chapter 14

Redemption Rock

For I know the thoughts that I think toward you, says the
Lord, thoughts of peace and not of evil, to give you
a future and a hope. —Jeremiah 29:11

After my dream of 1986 and the vision of the mountain, I prayed often in the hopes of gaining insight from the Lord as to its meaning and for direction in solving the problems of my sister's estate. I prayed *pretty much all the time*, but the timing was best when I mowed the lawn (with no interruptions and much time to think). We had a riding mower and nearly two acres of grass, so I spent a lot of time in prayer as I mowed. The grass needed mowing pretty much once a week, and it took 3–4 hours each time. You will see these hours of prayer and mowing were well spent as I tell you where we are today and what we have done.

The lawsuits are all settled, as well as problems with the IRS. We knew we had a lot of trespassers hiking up the mountain to *"The Rock,"* because of the fantastic view at the top. And, because *I felt the Lord had shared His broken heart with me* in the dream about "Still being rejected, going their own way, wickedness of the world," I wanted to remind people about God by having scriptures engraved on the rock. We were excited knowing we could share God's word without having to be there. We could remind the people trespassing about God, and perhaps make them happy, as well as the Lord.

We searched for a rock engraver, which turned out to be quite a challenge! We found a lot of engravers who would do it, but we had to bring the rock to them. We couldn't do that, as the rocks were too huge and attached to the mountain. There were several rocks and scriptures we wanted to use, mostly about the need to follow the Lord. Many scriptures would also be needed along the path to the top.

We finally found an engraver named Bill, who agreed to come there and do the engraving on-site. We all agreed on a day to start, and my husband, myself, and the engraver began the drive to the top. About halfway up, his pickup began overheating. He apologized and tried to fix it on the spot, but couldn't. He apologized again to us and said he would have to get his pickup fixed before he could come back again to begin. We knew this setback meant it probably wouldn't get done that year, and *we were sorely disappointed.* He said his goodbyes and started back down the mountain. I jokingly cried on my husband's shoulder, but with no tears. I was just making a statement of disappointment after being so happy, believing we were going to be able to honor the Lord with the engravings.

Suddenly, we saw the engraver speeding back up the road very fast. He drove right on past us and continued to the top. This time, he made it all the way up!

Journey to Redemption Rock

The first scripture complete was: "When my heart is overwhelmed within me, lead me to the rock which is higher than I" (Psalm 61:2). A few weeks after it was done, my husband and I noticed a small group of people standing on *"The Rock"* at the top of the mountain. We thought we should see who it was, since it is private property, so we hopped on our ATV and drove up the mountain. It turned out to be a youth group from a church in the Post Falls area. They were all quite happy and pleased with the engraving, because their youth minister had just preached a sermon about the *same* scripture that morning. We were happy also and felt it was the Lord's confirmation that the engravings were a good idea!

Bill could only engrave one scripture that first day, as it was getting late. We had to wait until the following year for him to finish the 11 engravings along the trail to the top. It turned out to be quite a task for him, hauling his sandblaster and heavy bags of sand up the trail.

There was a fairly good wind on one of the days he was working that was blowing his equipment, making his job even more difficult. He said a few choice words of disgust. *This was comical to us, to think of engraving scriptures and cussing while you were doing it.* I'm sure the Lord has been blessed by his work many times and may have even chuckled Himself. We will be forever grateful to Bill for his hard work and willingness of spirit. We are well pleased with his work!

We had one hiker who called me to say thank you. He said the hike to the rock made him feel like Moses, and that he had an incredibly good spiritual experience. Months later, he also rented the tower our son built up at the top. Our son named the tower Redemption Rock Tower. It is exceptionally beautiful and secluded, surrounded by windows, and the views are spectacular. The tower was completed after the Lodge was built.

We also thought it would be a good idea to create a place to stay for the people hiking up the mountain. So, we hired Rick Rieben to build a VRBO, Redemption Rock Lodge, for us below the mountain. It is about 5,200 square feet with 3 levels: a great room on the main level, a mini great room in a daylight basement, and a loft for a total of 5 bedrooms with extra bunk beds in the loft and mini great room. It has a wonderful kitchen on the main level and another one in the daylight basement, providing a workspace for more than one party. Since I am the mother of 5 married children and the grandmother of 12 and enjoy having family around me, we built it with family gatherings in mind and felt other mothers could benefit from having their families with them as well. The lodge is very comfortable for large extended family groups and will sleep 20. It has a fantastic view of the Rock, the valley, and incredible sunsets. We called the lodge and the tower *Redemption Rock*. The name is most appropriate, since we had to redeem most of the land from the county for our brother-in-law's delinquent property taxes. We have a great bear skin hanging on the dining room wall, compliments of the bear Rick Rieben hunted on our property.

We met Rick *by accident*—or *you might say God's coincidence*— when we were walking the property at the top. He asked us if he could hunt bear on our property. We said yes, and found out sometime later he went to our church and had a business of building homes. What a blessing that was! Turns out the Riebens are a wonderful Christian family, as well as great friends. They eventually bought 20 acres from us and invited their two daughters to build houses on their property. Rick also built a house further up the mountain for our son. It was completed in May of 2023, and he also built another house for our neighbors Ruth and Ken a short distance from us. We are so happy to have our son Steve living on the mountain. His house is also incredibly beautiful and has a spectacular view. Rick did an excellent job on all of the houses, and each was built to the specifications of each owner.

In 2023, we had a family gathering at the lodge with most of Shirley and Tom's children (except Denise, who had something else going on). It was a very fun day, and I'm sure there will be many more, as the lodge is a great place for families to gather!

Chapter 15

Troubling Phone Call With One Of The Daughters

Wisdom is the principal thing; therefore get wisdom. And in all your getting, get understanding. —Proverbs 4:7

I had a troubling phone call with one of Tom and Shirley's daughters about the deeds of trust her sisters and brothers had signed. These deeds were created at the request of the real estate company I had enlisted to sell the property at the onset of the problems surrounding the estate.

I realized she was not remembering certain events correctly and thought I could detect a possible misunderstanding of what had really happened, as well as some possible feelings of anger or bitterness toward some of her siblings. She mentioned how quickly they had signed the quitclaim deeds, relinquishing any rights they might possibly have as the children of Tom Wynecoop. She added that they signed them quickly because they thought, *"You were supposed to help us."* To be clear, they were not the owners on record (Tom was the owner), so it was not that they had any rights as heirs, but that they *might* have. Our conversation was very unsettling to me and hurt my heart, because previously she had assured me that she understood and had no bad feelings toward us.

I explained to her again, as I had tried to explain to all of Tom's children, that when we originally asked for their signatures for the quitclaim deeds, it was at the direction of the real estate company so they could list the land for sale. The real estate company said the land had to have a clear title in order to be sold. We also had to give the prospective buyer time to investigate the land and do any tests needed. *I worried time might be running out* for Tom to stay ahead of the creditors seeking to collect debts. After the deeds were signed and copies given to the real estate firm, the buyer they had mentioned was suddenly no longer interested and backed out, taking with him our hope of a solution for Tom's debts. I never saw him or spoke to him; I only knew of him through the real estate company.

What a disappointing and confusing time that was. I understand why the family was unhappy, and I was as well. *"Hope deferred makes the heart sick."*

Chapter 16

Trying To Help

Seek first the kingdom of God and His righteousness, and all these things shall be added to you. —Matthew 6:33

Some time ago, a very good friend called me expressing sorrow of heart and disappointment with the way the lives of those around him were going. He was depressed. His faith was wavering, and *a crack of doubt had slipped into his heart. Where was God? Was He still here?* He was sad because all the people he had been praying for were experiencing problems. *Why wasn't God helping?* He was pouring himself out trying to teach these loved ones God's words and God's ways, and it only appeared things were getting worse. They weren't listening, and some were still headed for destruction. *They were going their own way!* I felt bad for him as I listened and remembered a suffering Savior reaching out to a world that was STILL rejecting Him. I remembered Jesus working so hard to teach and warn a world that *couldn't care less.*

The people who crucified Him didn't want to hear about heaven or a promise of life after death, or the life-giving water that would give those who drank it "eternal life." The same people would, in a few short years, demand His death. This was an all-too-familiar story! Jesus prayed, "Father, forgive them, for they know not what they do."

Many religions recognize Jesus as a great teacher or prophet. But are they paying attention to His words today? Do we listen to the prophets that lived before the time of Jesus? Their prophecies are still valid. *Is the Teacher to blame because the student didn't listen...? Shall we blame God for all the wrong turns we take? Is God to blame if we drink and drive?* We have all heard the warnings about drugs, alcohol, and cigarettes! Now that people continue to use them and many suffer illness or disease as a result, *should we blame God? He's known as the Big Guy Upstairs, isn't He?* He's the man of miracles, right? *Isn't blaming God our way of removing the guilt from us? I think so!*

We are all responsible for what we choose to believe and the roads we take. We each must walk our own road of faith, seemingly alone at times, but we aren't walking alone. Yes, God will give us friends to walk with, and Scripture teaches that unseen angels help along the way. There are times I believe He removes our knowledge of His presence, for His own perfect reasons. My guess is that it is to test our hearts or build again on our faith in Him.

Sometimes the desire to change or rebuild comes after a storm that has passed through our lives or the lives of our friends and loved ones. We must not blame ourselves for what we or others are experiencing, *unless we have the power in our hands to change things.* We can only wait for the break in the storm, pray for them, love them, and pray that God will continue to provide us and them with seeds of faith to share with others *when our storehouse seems empty*.

Chapter 17

One More Miracle

His mother said to the servants,
"Whatever He says to you, do it." —John 2:5

It was a hot afternoon, and my son and I were driving into town to Post Falls without a care in the world, as it was a beautiful day. As we approached the corner of Holland Drive and South Stateline Road, my son slowed the car to make the turn onto Holland Road. As we pulled up to the stop sign, I thought I saw a little dust movement by the side of the road across the road to the left, about the distance of one or two blocks away. We made the turn, and as we got closer, the bit of dust now looked like smoke, so we stopped to investigate. What we thought was smoke turned out to be a cigar someone had tossed out of a car as they went by, and it was now turning from smoke to fire. We immediately called 911 and reported the fire.

The fire department came right away—I think it was probably 10 to 20 minutes. By that time, the fire was getting a pretty good start with the dry grass and a pine tree just a short distance from the road. The fire was approaching a nearby ranch and stable, and *we were incredibly happy* to see the fire trucks coming before it reached the stable and barn. I don't know if the owners had horses in the barn that day, but I'm sure God blessed them that day by having us report the fire when it was just a little smoke.

The owners were home, but not outside or in a place where they could see the fire starting. A few of the neighbors came out to see what was going on when they heard the fire truck's siren. There were several houses nearby that were in danger from the fire. Since it was a bit windy, and wind and fire are unpredictable, *I often wonder how much would have burned* had our son and I not been there—what direction and how far would the fire have spread? Since it was just a few blocks' distance from Stateline Road, with Washington on one side and Idaho on the other, would the fire have jumped the road? Would it have spread to the Washington side or Idaho? *Our son believes we may have saved land in Idaho and Washington at the same time.*

Just a few years ago, Steve's brother Dick and his wife Kay had to run for their lives, with fire right behind them. Their house burned, but their lives were spared. The fire had jumped the Spokane River and came very fast, as their house was right on the river's edge. They didn't have immediate neighbors, but luckily there were people with a vehicle nearby who came to help them escape the fire. *Second thoughts? I don't think that was luck either!* I think Dick and his wife Kay experienced a miracle also. Many of us do not recognize all the miracles God does in our lives.

At any rate, I thank God that He brought us there that day at Holland and South Stateline Roads, in time to spot the fire as a wisp of dust. Our vacation rental, Redemption Rock, was only 10 to 15 minutes away and could have been in danger also. *We were relieved we were there to see and prevent an unknown tragedy.* Would any lives have been lost? *I can't help wondering!* Only God knows and deserves our praises and gratitude.

Timing is everything to the Lord, and I am confident He had us there at the right time to save the neighborhood from a possible disaster. I recall the time long ago when the Lord and His mother Mary were invited to a wedding at Cana in Galilee. When the wedding ran out of wine, Jesus' mother Mary told Jesus, "They have no wine," and He replied, "My time has not yet come." (John 2:1–12).

Jesus hadn't planned to start doing miracles, but to honor her request and to meet the immediate need, He turned the water into wine. The governor of the feast called the bridegroom and said, "Every man at the beginning sets forth good wine; and when men have well drunk, then that which is worse; but you have kept the good wine until now." This was His first miracle He did at the wedding. Although it was unplanned, *I'm sure He rescued the host from a very embarrassing day.* This miracle manifested His power and glory by honoring the request of His mother—changing His timing to meet the immediate need. The scriptures teach us that God will sometimes change His plans as we pray, as He did with Nineveh. *"The blessings will come down as the prayers go up, so build your house on the Lord."*

Scripture teaches us that God was also very upset with how wicked the town of Nineveh had become and planned to destroy it. However, He wanted to give Nineveh a chance to repent and change her ways, so He sent the Prophet Jonah to warn the wicked city. At first, Jonah did not want to do it, because he knew God was merciful and would change His mind if they repented and changed, and he would look like a false prophet. *This is exactly what happened—Nineveh repented and was spared, and Jonah was temporarily mad at God and embarrassed.*

This recalls to mind my dream that Jesus was "still being rejected," "going their own way," and "wickedness of the world." *I don't think it would take a rocket scientist* to see how far off track our world has come. Let me encourage everyone to seek God about these three things and pray for God's wisdom and discernment. We know Jesus told us that one day this world will end, although "no man knows the hour or the day." We need to be talking to Jesus more and searching the scriptures, for He said, "These are they that testify of me." I encourage anyone who reads this book to accept Christ before He comes.

God has been striving to reach out to us since the beginning in the Old Testament, when He told Moses He would be "sending a great prophet." For Moses said, "I the Lord God will raise up for you a prophet like me from your own people; you must listen to everything He tells you." (Deuteronomy 18:15). And even Jesus said, "For if you believed in Moses, you would believe me; for he wrote of me. But if you do not believe his writings, how will you believe my words?" (John 5:46–47).

King David painted a picture of a suffering Christ in Psalm 22: *"My God, my God, why have you forsaken me?"* This Psalm was written about 600 years before Christ came. Isaiah paints another picture with his prophecy: *"He was despised and rejected by mankind, a man of suffering and familiar with pain."* (Isaiah 53). Most of this whole chapter describes Christ 700 years before He came.

I recall the Great Commission Jesus gave to His disciples before He ascended to Heaven. Then the eleven disciples went to Galilee, to the mountain Jesus had told them to go

Journey to Redemption Rock

to. When they saw Him, they worshiped Him; but some doubted. *(Remember doubting Thomas who had to touch the Lord's nail-scarred hands and put his hand in the sword wound in His side.)* Then Jesus came to them and said, *'All authority has been given to Me in heaven and on earth.'* (Matthew 28:18). "Therefore, go and make disciples of all nations, baptizing them in the name of the Father and of the Son and of the Holy Spirit, and teaching them to obey everything I have commanded you. And surely, I am with you always, to the very end of the world." (Matthew 28:19-20). "For God so loved the world, He gave His only begotten Son, that whosoever believed in Him would not perish but would have eternal life." (John 3:16).

Jesus cautions us, "Behold, I am coming as a thief. Blessed is he who watches and keeps his garments, lest he walk naked, and they see his shame." (Revelation 16:15).

Take care that you remain in Christ; *"I am the vine, you are the branches. He that abides in me and I in him brings forth much fruit; for without me you can do nothing."* (John 15:5). Most of all, let us not forget the warnings and the words of Christ—the one miracle above all miracles, the Son of God born of a virgin birth. We need to remember, Jesus said, *"Behold, I come quickly"* and *"I will be with you even to the end of the world."*

Just as Jesus declared on the cross, *"It is finished,"* signaling the completion of His earthly mission, so I declare these chapters of my journey to Redemption Rock complete.

The work He has set before me—to share this story of the *Journey to Redemption Rock,* a story of His Redemption and Faith—is now in your hands. *May it inspire you, challenge you, and draw you closer to the One who loves you beyond measure!* All glory and honor be to God.

Epilogue

*I have told you these things, so that in me you may have peace.
In this world you will have trouble. But take heart!
I have overcome the world. —John 16:33*

As I bring this story to a close, I am reminded of the countless ways God has woven His presence into the fabric of my life and the lives of those around me. This journey, filled with trials and triumphs, has been a testament to His unending faithfulness and grace.

From the moment of that profound dream in 1986, when I stood upon the mountain and met Jesus, to the realization of Redemption Rock, every step has been guided by His hand. The challenges we faced—the legal battles, the financial strains, the personal hardships—were all part of a greater tapestry that God was weaving for His purpose and glory.

Looking back, I see that our struggles were not in vain. They served to strengthen our faith, deepen our reliance on God, and refine our character. Just as gold is purified through fire, our trials purified our hearts and drew us closer to Him. We learned the true meaning of redemption—not just in the legal sense of reclaiming land but in the spiritual sense of being reclaimed by God. The land we fought so hard to save became a symbol of His redemptive work in our lives. Redemption Rock stands as a monument to His mercy and a beacon of hope for all who visit.

Throughout this journey, one theme has remained constant: the importance of unwavering faith in God. In times of uncertainty, when the path was shrouded in darkness, it was faith that illuminated our way. When we faced insurmountable obstacles, it was faith that moved mountains. Jesus said, *"If you have faith as a mustard seed, you will say to this mountain, 'Move from here to there,' and it will move; and nothing will be impossible for you"* (Matthew 17:20). Our experiences have proven this to be true. Even when our faith wavered, God remained steadfast, patiently guiding us back to Him.

Heeding the Call: A World in Need

The Scriptures are filled with calls to remember and obey God's word. Moses urged the Israelites to keep God's commandments and teach them to their children. The prophets warned of the consequences of turning away from God but also spoke of His unending mercy for those who return to Him. We are reminded of the prophecies of Isaiah, who described the Messiah as the Suffering Servant, bearing the sins of many (Isaiah 53). King David, in Psalm 22, vividly described the anguish of one forsaken, a foreshadowing of Christ's crucifixion.

Most importantly, we must not forget the words of Jesus Himself. He is the fulfillment of the Law and the Prophets, the embodiment of God's love and redemption. He warned us of the trials we would face but also promised His eternal presence and ultimate victory.

As I consider the state of our world, *I see parallels to the times of Noah, Moses, and the prophets—a world often consumed by selfishness, injustice, and a turning away from God.* Yet, in the midst of darkness, the light of Christ shines ever brighter. Jesus said, *"I am the light of the world. Whoever follows me will never walk in darkness but will have the light of life"* (John 8:12). It is our responsibility to reflect that light, to be ambassadors of His love, and to live out our faith authentically.

To those reading this book, I extend an invitation. *If you have not yet accepted Jesus Christ as your Lord and Savior, I encourage you to consider His offer of grace.* He stands at the door and knocks, waiting for you to invite Him into your heart (Revelation 3:20).

Salvation is not earned by our deeds but is a gift of God's grace through faith in Jesus Christ (Ephesians 2:8–9). No matter your past or present circumstances, *His love is available to you.* As the Apostle Paul wrote, *"If you declare with your mouth, 'Jesus is Lord,' and believe in your heart that God raised Him from the dead, you will be saved"* (Romans 10:9).

Living in Anticipation

Jesus promised, *"Surely I am coming quickly"* (Revelation 22:20). We do not know the day or hour, but we are called to be ready, living lives that honor Him and reflect His love to others. Remaining in Christ is essential, for He said, *"Apart from me you can do nothing"* (John 15:5). As we await His return, *let us be diligent in our faith, steadfast in our hope, and abundant in our love.* Let us forgive as we have been forgiven, serve as we have been served, and love as we have been loved.

I am filled with gratitude for the many ways God has intervened in my life. From the miraculous provision of our home to the redemption of the land, from the strength to endure hardships to the joy of seeing His promises fulfilled, He has been ever faithful.

I thank my family, friends, and all who have walked alongside me on this journey. Your support, prayers, and love have been invaluable. I especially thank my husband, Steve, whose partnership has been a source of strength and joy. Most of all, I thank my Lord and Savior, Jesus Christ. *His sacrifice on the cross, His victory over death, and His promise of eternal life are the foundation of my hope.*

"It Is Finished."

As I conclude this book, I leave you with the final blessing: *May you walk in the assurance of His love, the comfort of His presence, and the power of His Holy Spirit.*

Remember, *He who began a good work in you will carry it to completion until the day of Christ Jesus* (Philippians 1:6).

A hand-drawn portrait of Cottage Creek Inn, the beloved bed and breakfast operated by Jeanette and Steve Wynecoop from 1990 to 2020 — a place where countless memories were made and hospitality was a way of life. The portrait was drawn by Steve Wynecoop.

Redemption Rock on the horizon—a landmark that became a powerful symbol of hope, faith, and new beginnings.

Redemption Rock Lodge in Post Falls, Idaho—created as a place of gathering, restoration, and reflection, inspired by the enduring spirit of the Journey to Redemption Rock.

About the Author

Jeanette Wynecoop is a Pacific Northwest author and passionate storyteller whose profound faith serves as the foundation for all her work. In her debut memoir, *Journey to Redemption Rock*, Jeanette chronicles her powerful experiences navigating grief, loss, and complex legal battles following her sister's tragic passing. Her unwavering resolve to reclaim her family's cherished land is a testament to her deep spiritual convictions and resilience.

For thirty years, Jeanette and her husband, Steve, warmly welcomed guests from around the world to A Cottage Creek Inn, a tranquil five-room bed and breakfast embodying their commitment to faith, hospitality, and renewal. The lessons of comfort and connection cultivated at the inn deeply inform Jeanette's writing, offering readers solace, hope, and inspiration amidst life's challenges.

Beyond writing, Jeanette finds profound peace and clarity through immersing herself in scripture and exploring the serene beauty of Redemption Rock Mountain. Her mission is to empower others through her story, encouraging them to face adversity with courage and find redemption through faith and spiritual renewal. Jeanette continues to write, live, and inspire others from her home in the Pacific Northwest, guided by the transformative promise of a life aligned with Jesus Christ.

www.ingramcontent.com/pod-product-compliance
Lightning Source LLC
Chambersburg PA
CBHW020542080526
44583CB00013B/961